The Book

Getting the word out to know how we can stop Satan from stopping in Cleveland, Ohio at the time of the upcoming RNC with the information in the book. This has to be known by as many people as possible. Get the book, _Ending Political Wars in America_. Please help send whatever you can to pay for cost of television, radio, flyers to show people we can prevent the spiritual war that Satan's people on earth has promoted from hitting the ground and doing harm and destroying any part of the landscape it can.

The book has many things in mind to teach the political arena. First is to learn to get along in order to complete what may be on the agenda without all the backbiting. Second, to stop the upcoming process of what could become a riot or hands on fight between people who are out of touch with reality by way of a satanic presence that can and will make trouble from the chaos and confusion along with the disagreements that start up a kind of spiritual warfare that come down to earth.

Now if you can put aside what you believe or don't want to believe and don't think about this and let it be known as an imponderable/ponderable process people need to know that it expands in a state of reality and can affect people on earth.

At Bound to Heaven Publishing/Ministries, we are making things ready to have a good experience at the RNC for all involved and others in the surroundings community we are crossing all "t's" and dotting all "i's".

Welcome to a part of boundtoheaven.org. The writing I do for the filling up the people with food is the least I can do for the bellies of Christ.

There is a saying among some people who say heaven is only a stone's throw away. I question that but I do know in the wisdom the Lord gives me that Satan can be closer than people may think at time. Why do I say this? It is because when the prince of darkness strikes it has set in place a plan of action. And mankind knows this by way of the blessing of the Lord in his heart.

I am focusing on the upcoming convention in Cleveland and Philadelphia know there is a black cloud that is approaching them as fast as the people apply fear to the atmosphere, that can stop to stop the unseen black cloud that wants to rain down some kind of hell upon the people.

Thank God because at this stage we can stop the clouds and the process can be eliminated. How with the faith and belief we get as a part of the grace the Lord has around use with just because he loves us.

How can we get this done to stop the problem harm and damage that Satan wants to bring to the cities? The book titled with the brother to _Ending Political Wars in America_, titled _The Devil Passed Me By_, will also show the way to stop the crook so the black clouds we can't see will pass us by.

Be a Part of This

To foil of plan of Satan is one of mankind's greatest accomplishments. To know we are avoiding going to a dark place.

Now if people can create a restoration for the dome of the Capital Building in Washington, D.C. under budget and on time for the upcoming inauguration, we can create from love a rescue restoration for the people that start in their hearts is passed throughout the people that don't know so they will know.

The projects are backed by God's love in the presence of the believers. Keeping this in mind and bringing it to the people's attention this is not any kind of star war adventure. It is the real spirituality that makes a dimension or division of life complete.

To all: may this be known, the halo is over my head and the rainbow of peace and love is over the city of Cleveland, Ohio picture yourself with a halo over your head a picture of Cleveland with rainbows over it all in one.

We look forward to there not being a riot in Cleveland, Ohio.

This is something to think about as if you are an adult-kid or kid-adult, to take it in both ways not serious and serious at the same time.

It is Time to Know Now and to Know How

That we can stack the weapons to use against Satan to prosper mankind and that is our love for each other in a greater way and in greater numbers.

This information is spiritual therapy and it relates to the convention members and the public at large. The booklet helps to development a more compatible atmosphere. It provides a way for all to see within the City of Cleveland, Ohio that a spiritual wellness is here like a kind of ecumenical state of growth. Now, go figure.

Who Has All the Answers? Only Heaven Knows

The great part in and of life is you and we can hook our wagons on to each other and learn from one another.

To add an extra measure of success to your trip to Cleveland, Ohio, if you are participating in the RNC or not at that time, you may want to get a copy of the new book titled _Ending Political Wars in America_, by Bro. Tracy E. Bush. It tells of a way to give the utmost care about a level of newness, find peace to show the world how well behaved the people can be and it gives the power of insight to know how negativity or Satan can rain on the parade or storm on the focus of life in a greatly debatable place to enhance the level of trouble in a way to not get things done in a righteous and timely manner.

To have a better understanding of keeping the presence of darkness from coming into your acquaintance by hitching your wagon to a higher power that may help keep things safer and more productive for all involved in the political process of government and take a trip off the beaten path to gain a new perspective of insight that only could have been put in place by the good Lord if you are a believer. Get on this cloud of wisdom. Thank you for taking a new kind of challenge to create a better humanity and a better world, with boundtoheaven.org. Now who needs to add a different kind of safeguard to their life, we all do I hope and at the cost of a few pittance.

Who can afford to lose out on what could be a deal of a lifetime and possibly save some time and more so a life from danger at the same time. Again, to help reconstruct the plan with a more solid foundation between the earth and sky, this may be the deal of the century, believe it or not because you can't pay the cost for adding this what could be godly insurance to a growth stage in life without his approval and

4

that is who you can really thank for this. Amen and hallelujah.

One of the biggest reasons why it is a way to stop an unforeseen enemy and save a part of mankind's history that could have been harmed along with some people that may have been harmed also.

I think God's principals that gives a way to get out also the way of not becoming like some that may be a dirty rat fink kind of person that leaves them looking like a flea flicking fur bearing varmint. It is gentle persuasion that works with love to put the icing on the cake that can help stop an ungodly madness.

We Can Stop Satan's Building Process

Satan is building a cumulus cloud to put all of his weapons in that he is forming against the City of Cleveland at a special time in history. What does this mean? It is as simple as noting it and knowing people are saying it on television as well as Donald Trump also who are right there, the people who would rather fight than switch their allegiance in life to do what needs to be done.

Now we even have some who are promoting bad things to come to the City of Cleveland, Ohio on the web by selling t-shirts for up to $22.00 that is paying for them is promoting a riot. They are being promoted everywhere, television, radio, etc. Therefore, if it can get any sicker than that we are not going to let it.

That is why we are putting our combat skills to work to defend ourselves and stop the devil in his workshop and start laying off his workers as well as stopping his recruitment tactics.

Therefore, the cloud that is developing to loom over the city with all the weapons in it will be blown off course. The counteraction is in place to call for the north wind to get behind the City and blow the cloud of ill wind over the lake so the inhabitants within the cloud and all the weapons that has been formed against the people shall be shaken loose from the cloud and fall into the lake and shall be extinguished by the water in a kind of spiritual baptism that cannot be seen with the naked eye since the enemy comes with tools that are made up with fire. So the fire that is disguised as pain that wants to do harm cannot come against the people and the land.

We can, at the same time, release the blessings of the angels as a backup plan to the North wind, to call the cupids of love by way of the heavenly angels to release a barrage of arrows to assist the wind as it blows to deflate the ungodly from the clouds of people with egos that are a part of the on-cheerers on land to give them insight to stop raising hell with their blindness and darkness they carry around with them and in a lot of cases it is because of their own jealousy over someone else's blessings and they won't take time to try to develop their own or it is greed and the love of money.

To handle this will require stopping the madness. It won't pay off even if it appears to pay off for a short period of time. Therefore, if you are in this state of mind, don't force your hand against the will of the Lord. It is truly an unfit task to put upon yourself, because you can be changed in the twinkling of the sun when you open your eyes daily, in the name of Jesus.

If You Are One

If you are one of the people who think you can truly prosper from the use of your hands developing the tools of Satan that work against mankind, you are a lost people on the highways and byways that is caught up in the skyways by a personal spiritual war of self, with a lack of self-worth. Because of this you may follow a blind man off a cliff if he tells you we can fly. It is as simple as that. The true fact is the emptiness that causes pain in your life may be from not letting the Lord grow you up.

We must understand that to help stop the pain we must lose existing fear and stop creating fear. It is of a demon logic that is presented in the work you do for yourself gratification, and on a scale from 1-10, the precipitation of this kind of jaculation doesn't produce fruit to help replenish the earth. It only takes away from it and that leaves you with a zero. So take a break with a new level of understanding the power of love that you need to accept because if you don't change you may think it is a necessary wish. As a result you may become blind to ways to really be better off in this life and the next. In other words, do not let life get harder for you than putting a busted egg back together.

How long will it take to wake up people to the mountain of blessings that await us all become one who is of the truth to self and quit lying to self about the unrealistic part of their wisdom they preserve to outweigh the truth. Will the unwise side quit looking at themselves as if they can't do the wrong thing and stop following a dark pathway to a victory that has no meaning to the gift of life?

The Fight in the Sky

We are just the on-thinkers because we cannot see it, but it is greater than the thriller in Manilla. To keep cheering it on means to keep cheering the victory of it where God has stepped in to replace us in this fight, we must stay prayed up and full of cheer and enjoy the peace that the weapons cannot prosper and all clouds have been removed from above the places which was once projected to hold the darkness within. Now let's keep it simple and not be simple.

Out of All I Have Been and Done, No One Has a Reason to Speak Against this Work!

I have a few recommendations that I think will enhance the development of growth as it is already being developed to continue to secure the homeland in which we live, but also to secure a better understanding of what part any and everyone who is exposed to this information can have in making this a more pleasant developmental process of growth for the country.

This Goes for Any Gathering That May Have Some Kind of Opposition

This information is especially for anyone who is to be a part of the protests that could occur outside of the RNC location. The more informed you are the better off all at the event will be.

This gives a humanitarian presence that can be shared in spirit, to keep everyone in a peaceful and serene state of mind and to know you can and are being guided and guarded by love.

Why do some people act like a fool and others don't? It could be a number of reasons that set people off and at the same time it could be a number of reasons that keeps some people calm and cool under pressure.

Now if we can summarize it or put it in a nutshell, we will say it is the lack of being grounded that takes some people out of the right element and we can say it is the weight that some people carry around with them, while it is going on. What do I mean exactly? It is the non-ability to keep one's feet planted on solid ground. It is as if one person has such heavy load and when something upsets them, they go off or they may be looking for this to happen to take the pressure and weight off of them that is the kind of person that may lose control at a function.

It is like something in the atmosphere controls them, which could be Satan and if they are in an unknown spiritual war of any kind that may spell out trouble. It can be stopped by identifying it and then stopping the fear of the unseen but known enemy

Now, for the cool hand that can be developed by all people if they don't have it already it is someone and not them trying to keep themselves level all of the time because they believe that the Lord has their balance. The weight they carry around won't let them down like others. Therefore, they are not affected by the atmosphere of Satan and the darkness and trouble can't take them and put them in a troubled state of mind that makes them want to do the wrong thing. They have sense enough to get out of the way if and when it comes so it is not so hard to crack a nut in one's self before you become one.

The creation of this came by way of a motivation to keep the people and the city of Cleveland, Ohio along with Philadelphia, PA safe and content over the process of the convention but the same principals can be used over and over again.

Take the preparation and put them in the forefront of your mind before you go to the place where you will be only participating in airing out your point of view with others knowing it is not a boxing match or a fight of any kind.

It is a respectful gathering of protest to be heard and let lots of people know how you feel. If anyone else wants to make something else out of it other than that, they need to go home or to jail.

How to Handle Confrontation
Plain and Simple as THIS

Walk away the face to face shouting match you don't go there if someone wants to cause a scene like that move to another area and don't look back or go back and if a person insists on trying to make a scene with you, do the right thing. Alert the law enforcement about who it is and point them out.

There are right ways and wrong ways to do things and you have the choice to do the right thing. It is a commitment in your heart and no power on earth can change that once you have made up your mind in the presence of the Lord if it is right. Know that will give you all the confidence you need thanks to the Lord. Peace in and peace out all over.

These are Facts

These are facts to help people to better understand themselves. The process of common courtesy is the way we are supposed to behave and if you step on someone's toes you should automatically apologize.

This is a fine way to be but at a point if you are in an area where someone keeps doing it and don't have the "it" factor of being a gentle man or woman; you may as I said leave or look at them as a sick person.

What can we do for the sick? Pray ahead of time and carry a sense of pride in the sincerity we have in ourselves. This is what that will consist of our imagination that is on alert and give us a perception in a vision that at this place and time we are at and with all that may be going on we have an outlook from top to bottom.

Within the outlook it is always and constantly be sprinkled with a burst of Holy water that is being released by a cloud in the presence that gives the armor to the people to keep cool and protect themselves with knowledge they are also protecting others.

This presence comes by way of the angels that have been dispatched in the land of the lake of love that we possess in our hearts and the more who possess it the more angels will be there to keep us safe and filled up with peace.

Now, our biggest presence to stop the part of hell that wants to rise up at a time like this is fear and since fear is stripped down to its lowest form, it is nothing in the presence of people that have a heart of stone love that won't let the enemy in to break it up or tear it down, no matter how it tries.

Raising Air; Ending Fear

If hell is below then turn fear around because it tries to scare people off of the earth to make them come there and the Lord is the ruler of the sky so let's take things to another height.

Ending Note

Have I been approached or tried in a position that gave me a reason to go off or is it said from 0-100 and I had the first mind or the gut feeling to walk away until I went on and left. Where did this happen? At a rally that was at the front entrance of the Justice Center in Cleveland, Ohio in 2015.

I was the there to bring a point out that if both parties are looking for a peaceful solution I have suggestions in the book titled *A Peace Offering for the Police and the People.* I had a friend with me and he also was approached by some people there were retaliators or rebel-rousers and they didn't like the fact of me being there and trying to rise up some kind of hell from the grave of someone who is dead.

To honor the dead I know this was there only inward pathway to choose me and what I had to offer the peace making process and it could have gotten not so nice. I wasn't a coward about it but to show respect, I left. It took that to keep the peace and I was glad to do it because these people were in a spiritual war with themselves and all they needed was an excuse to create trouble. That is not what life is about. It is a love thing and people forget that too often. Don't be one who forgets about love.

If you can learn anything out of this, learn to become a person who doesn't blindly look at the truth and ignore it or refuse to see it because if you do witness it one day you may wish you were blind.

At Bound to Heaven Publishing/Ministries, we are allowing you to get the best protection that you can, using methods that are made up of love.

To help make things clear, we have been in contact with the Cleveland police and U.S. Secret Service, the local clergy, media, as well as local residents and politicians on many levels.

In saying this, the book may also help in the line of homeland security and secret service.

At Bound to Heaven Publishing/Ministries we are doing what it takes to level the playing field in life so everyone has a chance to play center but become a pitcher also to help them hit a home run with their life.

To anyone who has the ability to read and perceive this understanding, you are personally certified to become a peacemaker that will avoid harm because you do not harm. This is the principals walking with a holistic view of reality and holiness in the way you live your life.

Let the Lord

Catch you before you try to; It is better for all.

Watch the Atmosphere

It does change on your behalf no buts about it.

We Take Enough

Of our own punishment we put on ourselves unknowingly in life, at times to the point we need not give in to adding more to it we can prevent.

Togetherness

We can champion the causes that are larger than ourselves if we work together.

People you can stop living off of being ignorance and try some real blessings.

A Wake up Call

There comes a time that there should be one in history, as if it is upon the same pathway as once upon a time there was an undertaking of the properties of nature that came under fire in a time of revolution to supply Americans with resources that came from the woods that tore apart the forces, in some of the most beautiful places. Then mankind had to step in to stop the madness and repair the landscape.

Well, it is a divine kind of precursor that is or has been taking place on the destruction of mankind that needs a new kind of guideline to repair the landscape in man's mental crossover to give him insight to cross back over to a land inside of himself where it is safe.

There is no need to totally explain why it is time to be blessed with the why not. Why not go to a safe place where the unknown part of the prince of darkness cannot go to cause any more pain in life than a person has coming their way anyway.

If I need to go from a to z, it still does not mean as much as it can because we are on a pathway alike and not alike. The key to all pathways inside one's self is the learning of the presence of your surroundings and this is different in everyone. One thing remains, the road once discovered to stay on that gives light is of virtue that increases love all around you.

Therefore in a way we grow to make us capable of learning to unveil ourselves from darkness with daylight and share this with others. This, I feel has been somewhat lost in a new level of revelation of the inner connections of space and time that is good in one way but disconnects us from ourselves that has been taking place in America. That is why before we miss out on the development of a part of ourselves that has had its own hard enough time, looking forward to a daily growth with mankind. It needs to be looked at closer and rediscovered to give more guidance and love to the world and its people.

We need to put more research in spiritual skills that can help deliver us out of darkness in a time that we have so much daylight to be shared. The use of them will take life skills to another level. That will create a godly revolution.

That is why I implore you to try it and see if we want to show the rest of the world that we have not fallen as far behind as it is shown to them. Why not go for it and look at what we can gain that can become a part of all of our other accomplishments. If you truly believe that there is a love for this new country we live in and it can be made to live up to what it wants to appear to be, start today without hesitation and believe you are not alone. Believe there is a multitude of people who are on the same accord. We the people are starting off fresh as if we have discovered a way to give the land we live in a rebirth of it.

The part of the land I am talking about is two sided as a coin; the one side is within the land of self. The other side is outside of us in the land we live in, along with the atmosphere and the way we will be treating it from now on.

How much more can I say to you that you have not heard before? If there is anything new it is of the power of the most high that it has come from. It has taken me over two thirds of my life to get to a place where I am hoping someone is listening and more so acting on the wisdom for God's sake because it is from him I know in my heart that he gives me the life to keep going to the inkwell to work my hand and heart on paper.

Therefore may the words I have be a part of constructing a lighthouse to not only show you his way but give you the insight to one day build one of these for others to see just as the Lord has plans for you to do.

One question I have is: have we grown enough? Or are we more so afraid of the old frontier of spiritual enlightenment that we feel it to be a threat to our personal well-being as if we do not believe it wants to exist. Therefore, we can determine what kind of future awaits us when we die. Well, I say if that is so then why did someone want to become human, if there was a choice, and they feel they have done so many things even though I cannot think of one, can you?

A Poem

It is nice to have faith in my fellow man. It is delightful to believe in my people who I share a life force with. It is just a thought of not knowing if there is any other place that exists around that I can see of or know of other than heaven. That is why it is nice to know I have you. It is the will of man to choose his destiny. I like to entrust mine to the Lord.

Through an Action of Kindness

What have I done lately that gives me notification that this has a chance to work in helping to stop a glimmer of uprising that may lead to violence at a protest? I have helped to create hope with an ounce of prevention with an anticipated outcome of a pound of cure. A great deal of this is about the disconnection of a mob mentality.

In retrospect of the thought, if I were a kind of demi god-minded person, it was not of my own doing. The point in saying all of this can touch home and bring about a change. I have the tools I have been given in many different ways when I placed a billboard kiosk in front of the Justice Center in Cleveland, Ohio during the time when the police and people were clashing. Did it help when I gave away free copies of _The Forerunner to A Peace Offering for the Police and the People_, along with promoting it around the country, in just about every major city that assured the main ones with problems received it, even though I got to some after the problem had escalated. Just the same, did it have an effect on the people and landscape of thought that someone cares and is trying to help? I think it did and that is why I am at it as always, trying to make it better and giving people something to help them come to a better reality and conclusion about an act of violence and raising some kind of hell.

Therefore, if I made it known that you can help others better by helping yourself first, and if you don't know how, there is a way down inside of you that can come out if you give it a chance. That is the blessing that can be looked for and found. This takes us all back to each one, teach one. If you are the first one, it only takes one more. It is not complicated and can be made simple if you give the wisdom a chance to sink into your life and let some of it do the thinking for you. To help with that part, try meditating and making goals that say, "Lord let your wisdom do my thinking for me. Let your will become a part of my will. Let the actions in me not be guided by my emotions but by the presence of you in me that I inherited on the day of resurrection, after you died on the cross."

Try that as an example of protection that can grow your love for life on all levels in a presence of newness that fills you up and it will cause your cup to overflow, with delight that gives the presence of God's grace walking in front of you, beside you, in back of you, most of all inside of you. Therefore, how can someone not take this as a challenge that will let you see the defeat of Satan out of your presence?

As far as the promotions to help prevent riots which could help the RNC or the DNC, it could not contain the presence of a wildfire that has gotten started, but it can be a kind of containment field put up around the two locations if it is set in place in time. It may sound kind of star warrish, but the act of a presence of a godliness that is watching over the land and people to stop the fear that builds the uncontrollable negativity and urges to want trouble that is inspired by Satan inside of people can be suppressed.

The suppression of this that keeps people's feet planted on solid ground where they cannot be caught off guard and sucked into the atmosphere of the spirit of Satan that promotes warfare, can be stopped.

The tools have been given to mankind by the Lord. More than one person has them. Now who will mankind choose to show people how to use them, and is mankind still too smart to use what the Lord has for them or will he, in this case, rely on his own kind of infinite wisdom that he creates in and for himself without a lead he takes from the Lord. Well, we will see.

If There Has Been Anyone

If there has been anyone who has been in the world for any amount of time, it is a given that you know your faith does exist. Therefore, it is a gift to you that you can accept if you choose. Another one of the mustard seeds of faith that is presented by the Comforter as a way to know of the power to step out of the box or comfort zone that may be keeping you blinded.

This chapter is yours to turn as often as you need to in order to bring order to your life and the loved ones around you. It is there to put your faith and belief to work without the fuss and must that some put in front of change to persuade them not to do anything. It can give you the ability to know when your foresight is kicking in to warn of danger. It can give you the power to stay on the right side of the line in order to not step in a place where serpents lie, in wait to do harm. It can give the vision of tomorrow that may surpass today's understanding with this seed of faith that is of a divine order that mankind will be able to cherish with his heart and soul.

The valuable parts of our spiritual economy comes with a cost that is paid for with study and faith in the works that has to be done in someone and out of them, so the world can see. Thank God that it is a shift in the atmosphere and the ill wind is blowing out to sea.

Take Time Out to Pass Along This Information to All Politicians

There is not enough to be said about the big draw to possible major problem at the convention that has people in a somewhat déjà vu because people don't know about towerism that a large number don't know they have this also.

This can be found in the book *Fixing What is Broken in America*

The Tricks of the Process

The tricks are in the process that Satan takes some people who take him for granted the ones who think they know enough about him to play inside of his fire. They may be the one who he sets up on a pedestal to make them feel good about what they do. More so he puts all the love they need in their life in a way that blinds them because they would have gotten it anyway. It makes the person think they have to have it all to keep them who may be there so they pay the cost to the demon way of living to keep them in a presence of wealth. They get so high off of this kind of life they would rather die than give it up.

They get the same treatment that Eve got an apple that makes them feel their life is so set it blinds them more to a level of non-reality existence they can see and subconsciously they feel as they are a demi-god. Once there it is the place that comes along with the title of being a towerist.

Then without the true perspective of what is going on in one's self and the heart repenting before the mind does it, they get stuck and it becomes a lost pathway that gets harder and harder to come out of, unless you get a blessing of a special kind and the only one I know of comes from the freedom that the word of God can supply to give the light out of this kind of darkness.

That is what this writing can do if someone lets it, if they are there. To help you come down from within that dark cloud, you can by reading and studying *Fixing What is Broken in America*.

The Danger of It

What a euphoric feeling that people feed themselves up with the endorphins that come from their own inner nature that supplies them that will get them a personal high feeling of their own production. This is dangerous because it leaves the Lord out of a presence in a person that can and will keep them blinded to the truth.

We Can do it Together

Stop the madness that leads to sadness and harm and pain. We can lose the mob mentality. We can leave the protest or rally as if we were at a fellowship gathering in love and peace. Now will we speak for the people and earth?

Satan Has a Game Plan

One of his biggest cons is he knows that people are hurting and some are so desperate for love they will fall for anything. Truth, not fiction, and what he does is use this factor on a reverse level of phycology to trick people to believe that is what they got coming when they follow his lead. If you are blind to the real reality of the love that the Lord supplies.

It is open season for you to get got by him and he has more ways to do this than anyone can think about. Therefore, be careful of a dark love trap. It can snap on you and make you snap.

We Should Know By Now

When resources dry up, people collapse and that is why we are replenishing the power source in the spiritually wounded's hearts and minds and spirits, of the human side of life along with the non-human side that keeps the spiritual being inside of the earthly body safe.

We don't have to keep going to a dry well. Change the well or if the life water is not good, change the well. Within a new well we can change our ashes into diamonds.

We All

We all want to connect with something and develop something with our roots that we leave for future generations. That is what we do in the human experience as long as we do not create a disruption in the lives of self and others that creates a loss that adds pain and agony. That may seem like it is not a big thing but in the grand scheme of things, it is.

It is placed inside of you now according to the will the Lord has in you for his purpose and this is the only rule that is or comes up about it that lets it soar up and if need be, show how it is done in the spirit by way of the flesh. This gives a sense of control of protection in one's self like no other can do. It is now to know of it to see it for yourself.

Foremost, the violent levels of people in a crowd that can separate and stay in place and in peace you should look forward to that in the USA we will not display anymore where it is not to be because we are free of Satan's grip in this manner of existence.

This is a part of the boomerang effect. Throw it out and get more back.

We Can and Do Retool for Better Rules

People need to stop worrying; it fuels fires. Now who can accept the truth or are we a people who have been so blinded in some ways that we can't accept it? Some people may have an inner need to see some kind of hell break out.

But, as a reassurance, the ideal people won't go there since they have accepted the Lord. At the same time, would like to see a part of it?

What don't they do? They don't support the right cause. They look for justice after they do nothing to stop the injustice. If that is not enough to make you a little sick, nothing will. But God can fix that too. Thank you for lending your ear.

This is a little diddy of a truth helper of the Lord.

The Pissy Skunk Syndrome

We can't afford to not inform people to not get into a pissing war with a skunk; they can't win!

Well, if that be who some are it is a shame because they may be also some kind of skunk that offends the Lord's nostrils and they don't know it. I pity the fool that doesn't know they are one, especially the educated ones, because they make up the worse kind, because it seems like some may never learn.

The stinking thinking even gives a way to people who won't mind getting business off of something others tear up. Note: there is still hope and help for you; ask the Lord to forgive you for your way of thinking also you must forgive yourself and others. Then see the change that takes place in your life for the better.

We Can't Afford to Let This Influence Anyone!

This could be an ideal card to carry around with you as a reminder to you to just say "No!" Don't be a skunk because we have seen enough of this in the candidates who are pissing on each other!

Could this idea or be a labor that is only for the people that have no unrest in the place where the convention is held? The uptown people may feel like this because if they have no reason to be down there and no kind of investment other than to see who comes out the winner, they may have a backup plan to a point they feel one way or the other the newly elected president will not stop much of their progress in life.

This may be what is called self-taught therapy that increases self-grown love that so many people are in need of. There are some not so pleasant parts about life we can change and not get used to. This was just another one but if we keep the right attitude and say we can eliminate them or the possessiveness about whatever they think can do. We can help end a lot of that kind of thing that helps stop any kind of hater out in the world.

Now to put it in a nutshell and keep it there the actions that come about is a pathway that humans go on to try to get things done. But if the traps have set they wind up on a different one that has a surprising ending. That is why we have developed the skills to keep you on track because no one really means to wind up in the void-noid pathway that Satan has put up a sign that is flashing but it is a setup to trip up anyone it can that will bring about a not so good present and ending to a day that doesn't have to have the kind of wrinkle in it or troubled water someone may have to maneuver out of.

Therefore, keep your eyes on the prize to not lose your way and beware of the void-noid because it is a place that creates self-sabotage. That makes problems that you can avoid pop up and somewhat appear out of nowhere. So take a hold of the treatment is supplied by the Lord and use it if needed because you can't beat it.

We are learning to show it is better to give than to receive

We are at our best when we are in agreement

We can come to the best part of life when we know the Lord

We can learn not to stray too far into and through dark pathways

The world needs to know they can be free of Satan's grip.

When

The world keeps trying to get you down you just keep making them out of a clown. Laughter can be some of the best medicine.

Love = **L**imited or **L**ongsuffering
Off or **O**n
Victim or **V**ictorious
Ended or **E**ndless

Carry This in Your Heart

This information shows a way of protesting without having violence at the protests!

I am a personal protester of non-violence and I will not participate in it. I will not condone it. I will not act in it. I will not be a part of it. I pledge this before my Lord and the world to become a peacemaker who lives with love in my mind, heart and soul. This love is guided and guarded by my spirit in conjunction with the Spirit of God.

This is another little book that helps take a big bite out of crime

If you find something that I wrote that got your goat, make a note and if you like, you can let me know.

_____

_____

_____

_____

_____

_____

_____

_____

_____

_____

_____

_____

_____

_____

_____

_____

_____

_____

_____

_____

_____

_____

_____

_____

_____

Philippians 4:17

17. Not that I seek the gift, but I seek the fruit that abounds to your account.

Acts 20:24

24. But none of these things move me; nor do I count my life dear to myself, so that I may finish my race with joy, and the ministry which I received from the Lord Jesus, to testify to the gospel of the grace of God.